Teaching of History in Schools

Dr. Masroor Hashmi
Retired Dean Faculty of Education
Jamia Millia Islamia, New Delhi

PREFACE

This is the English translation of my Urdu book. Urdu book was published in 1975 when I was a lecturer in Teaching of History in Teachers College, Jamia Millia Islamia, New Delhi. The Urdu book was reprinted in 2011.

Every school teaching subject has four dimensions: objectives, teaching methods, curriculum, and evaluation, around which all knowledge of teaching that subject is communicated. Though there are chapters more than the needed four in this book the extra chapters have been added for their relevance to the subject of history.

People indulge in discussions about the need of including history in school curriculum. However, history itself has established its need by continuing its single or partial inclusion in school curriculum. Let us remember that cultures and civilizations have emerged from their past and so have a history. If we want our oncoming generations to know their cultural, social, and economic roots we have to transmit the knowledge of their history, and earlier it is done in their educational phase the better. Hence the need of teaching history at school stage.

Examples are given from medieval history of India at different place in this book. I have done my masters in medieval Indian history, and naturally feel comfortable to give examples from that period. But the subject of this book is not history as such, it is teaching of history. Student teachers can replace examples of medieval Indian History by examples of any other period of Indian history.

Thanks are due to my son Syed Irfan Hashmi and my grandson Syed Hashir Hashmi who helped me to relearn the use of computer.

Dr. Masroor Hashmi
Charlotte, NC

May14, 2017

Table of Contents

Chapter 1: What is History? 1

Chapter 2: Importance of history and its objectives 9

Chapter 3: Method of teaching: Lecture method 17

Chapter 4: Method of Teaching: Source Method 23

Chapter 5: Dalton Plan and Project Method 29

Chapter 6: Curriculum 38

Chapter 7: Textbook of History 44

Chapter 8: Evaluation in History 49

Chapter 9: Preparation of Lesson Plan; Some Specimen Lesson Plans ...56

Chapter 10: Communalism and Writing of History in Modern India 69

Chapter 1: What is History?

History of History

The word historia was given by the fifteenth century B.C.Greek historian Herodotus. Its meaning is investigation, search etc. Herodotus has written history in the manner of storytelling and has emphasized observation. He wrote whatever he observed. On the contrary a contemporary historian Thucydides has viewed historical events quite critically. History written by Thucydides provide many lessons to politics. The manner of his writing is quite didactic. These two historians had charted two different ways of writing history. Writing of history continued on these two ways of writing for 2200 years. Histories written on the style of Herodotus are very interesting, because they are written in story telling style. Histories written on the style of Thucydides provide political wisdom to contemporary politicians

Style of history writing changed in the nineteenth century. Leopold Van Ranke, a teacher in a German secondary school, introduced a new style of writing history. Those were the days when Europe was passing through industrial, agricultural, political, and religious revolutions and public mode of thinking was changing. Ranke neither wanted to discuss past nor its relations with the present. To him the purpose of writing history was simply to narrate whatever had happened in the past. Interpreted in German language it meant "wie es eigentlich gewesen" Ranke's approach was quite convincing, so people tried to adopt his outlook. Many people beside Ranke adopted different approaches to writing of history. Some appreciated the didactic approach of Thucydides, others appreciated Gibbon. Some disliked the scientific approach of history writing because it overlooked the moral aspect of history. Some were in favour of keeping history a part of literature. There were storytelling historians and followers of Thucydides as well during this century. History writers who adopted the approach of Thucydides were liked because of some social and political movements during that century. Their histories provided insight for contemporary politics. H.T.Buckle was a critic of Ranke. He thought that collecting facts of history was of course worthy of appreciation, but at the same time it was also necessary to make generalizations on their basis. Generalizations cannot be omitted in subjects of study which have provision for research. How can history be an exception for not making generalization, he argued. But generalizations of the type of chemistry and physics cannot be made in history.

The concept of history given by Ranke was full of great men of their times. History could be written through the achievements of great men. This was very much criticized. Earlier in the eighteenth-century Voltaire had given the concept of world culture. German historians had given the concept of "kulturgeschichte" which meant that great men could interpret the ideas and sentiments through their sayings and actions, and this is their greatness. But it was wrong to say that a person could represent an entire period. This concept overcame the concept of Ranke, and people who believed this concept tried to find out through research the ideas, feelings and actions which were popular or were influencing people during a period.

Search for a proper definition

Many people have tried to define history. Authors, generals, kings and politicians have defined history in their own way. Napoleon stated that every story that has public acceptance becomes history. Froude has defined history in a poetic manner "it is a sound echoing for centuries in the corridors of time." A simple definition is that every past event becomes history, and entire human past is history.

To understand properly the definition of history we must try to understand past events in their proper background. For this purpose, we should study events with the help of a suitable method so that we may reach a conclusion and be able to define history ourselves.

The things that help us collecting historical events are called "sources ". It would be a little funny to say that human beings are also a source of history. But all would agree that habits, manners, languages, traditions, and manner of living can help us learn about human past.

Sources can be divided into two major categories. One, that are called "traditions". Two, that are called "remains". Traditions can be further divided into three categories: oral traditions, written traditions, pictorial traditions. Oral traditions are those stories and poems which are related to past events and are transferred from generation to generation. Written traditions are writings on stones and various type of papers. Pictorial traditions are cave inscriptions, paper or wall paintings. All these traditions have been left consciously by past generations for future generations. Remains are those things which people of past generations have left unconsciously in language, literature, art, Industry, law, and rituals. Remains can help us in understanding food, dress, manners, and style of living of past generations, and also their words, phrases, and values.

Sources can be divided into two categories from the point of view of their importance: primary sources and secondary sources. Primary are those sources which provide facts of history directly such as ancients habitations, forts, tombs, coins, laws, edicts, decrees. The histories compiled with the help of primary sources are called secondary sources. For example, old fort, qutub minar, and other monuments of Delhi are primary sources and the book Asar-us-Sanadid by Sir Syed Ahmad Khan is a secondary source.

Sources before Egyptian civilization, Babylonian civilization, Chinese civilization, and Indus valley civilization are many. They are so simple that we never think to know their origin. We do not know who made bow and arrow? Who produced fire? Who domesticated animals and birds? It would be wastage of time to make a list of such things which play an important role in modern life but their originator is not known to us.

Sources are studied in a technical manner. Let us take written sources to learn the "historical method" with the help of which we work with sources. Historical method is composed of two processes, analysis and synthesis. Suppose we are working on an old book written by someone who happened to live during the times of recorded events. The first part of analysis which is denoted as external criticism will start with checking the authenticity of the book. External criticism provides the information about date or time of the book, the place where the book was written, the conditions under which the book was written. Internal criticism starts after external criticism. The reader of the book puts himself in the position of the author of the book and tries to collect information about the conditions surrounding the author of the book, his manner of thinking, does his words conveying the same meanings as we understand them? Was he in a position to know the events? Were his observations correct? Did he write exactly the same as he observed?

Some other facts come to light after being satisfied with the authenticity of the book through analysis. Then starts the second process, synthesis. Conclusions drawn from the facts thus collected and facts themselves are then written in an organized manner.

Facts provide the basis of the twin process of analysis and synthesis. It is therefore, necessary to write a few things about facts of history. Facts are selected for different reasons. Sometimes those facts are selected which are interesting and can be remembered easily. Sometimes facts are selected to serve politics, trade, religion, or education. Evidently in such cases only that aspect of life would be visible on whose basis facts are selected. Our point of view for selection of facts should be a holistic view of the past, and its relationship with the present. Understanding past and establishing its relationship with the present comes under the concept of evolution. History is the record of human evolution, and we have to select facts of history with this point of view. Let it be clear in our mind that evolution does not mean development. Development means good and interesting changes, whereas evolution might be composed of both good and bad changes.

Is history science?

It has been discussed for a long time whether history is art or science. An account of historical method was given in the preceding pages. Traditions were criticized in it from bygone days. Criticism was used by Muslim scholars while collecting the sayings of the Prophet. Historians of European renaissance also used it. This process of historical criticism points towards the efforts of the past for developing history as a science.

The discussion that history is science or art started with historical criticism. History remained a part of literature so long as it was supporting the contemporary politics. The stories of brave hearts of Greek city states narrated with exaggeration were considered part of history. That was the time when poets and storytellers were considered historians. This relationship between history and literature continued for centuries.

In the nineteenth century when science dominated every aspect of human life temperament of history also changed. The discussion whether history is science or literature changed as a consequence of this change. So long as history was considered a part of literature the need for its definition was not felt. But when it came abreast with science need for its definition arose. History is a science but not of the type physics or chemistry are.

The method to reach truth in history is scientific. But it is difficult to observe the material of history directly because all the events have happened in the past. On the contrary conclusions may be reached through observations in physics, chemistry and biology. In history efforts are made to reach conclusions with the help of writings of past authors or monuments and other sources. The similarity between methods of science and history is search for truth. Both methods emphasize objectivity, but subjectivity can be controlled in physics and chemistry not in history.

Screening the facts of history

To accept a historical fact, it is necessary to have at least two witnesses in its support. These two witnesses may be two documents, two decrees or two books. After the acceptance of a historical fact the second thing is to assess its true importance. There is much scope of difference in doing so. A historical fact may be important for one historian and may not be so important for another. The difference depends largely on the social and political background of the two historians. Sometimes historical facts are important for one generation and not so important for the succeeding generation. Sometimes because of difference of purpose historians give two versions of a historical fact. It therefore, becomes very difficult to say how important is a historical fact. But it does not mean that because of such difficulties we should put aside efforts to judge the importance of a historical fact. It becomes all the more necessary to assess the true importance of a historical fact despite these differences.

German origin historian Henry Rickert has worked on historical method. He admits the necessity of screening the truly important facts, but a historian cannot screen the facts like a scientist because facts of history and facts of science are basically different. But with the enlargement of the meaning of science historical facts also came under its range. Then efforts were made to search the standards which could help in assessing the importance of historical facts.

Two standards were made for that purpose. One, how important was a historical fact for the people of those times. Two, what was the relevance of a historical fact for present times. Ranke was in favour of the first standard because only then history could come nearer science. But, he argued, that it should be done with utmost objectivity. His view was appreciated for a long time because he had shown a new solution of the problem of writing history. But in the beginning of the twentieth century historians started saying that subjectivity cannot be totally controlled in history writing. Since history writing cannot be shorn of subjectivity we must not be so much against subjectivity. Consequently, element of subjectivity increased in histories written afterwards. James Harvey intervened in the dispute and opined in 1912 that we should not advise historians in their judgements regarding selection of facts. Let them select the facts they genuinely feel proper.

Setting principles in history

History writing has changed many a times. Sometimes facts were reformed and history writing changed in the light of new facts. Sometimes, old facts were changed by new facts and changed thinking modes affected history writing. But nobody can deny that history has always been the reflection of evolution process and has always been dependent on research. It has always been a record of past and past events have always been the content of history. It is true that historians paint history in the colour of their beliefs. Since historians live in present times and are affected by their political, social, economic and cultural environment they look past events in the light of present times.

To overcome this shortcoming and to bring history nearer

science efforts were made to frame principles which may separate the colours of historical rainbow. Edward P. Cheyney assumed the following principles in 1923. He thought that those principles could provide guidance to writers and readers of history. We can be guided by those principles with a disclaimer that they were based on assumption and were not the result of research.

1. Principle of continuity: human life continues despite obstacles
2. Principle of change: changes happen in all times
3. Principle of mutual dependence: people flourish under it
4. Principle of democracy: process of life becomes democratic
5. Principle of freedom of expression: oppression brings destruction
6. Principle of moral development: moral development dominates material effects

Apparently, it seems that all historical material can come within the scope of these principles. But as has been mentioned earlier these principles have not been judged on the basis of research so no judgement can be given about them.

Questions:
1. How far do you agree with the ideas of Leopold Von Ranke regarding history writing?
2. Which things you keep in mind when reading sources.
3. What is your opinion about history, is it science or literature?
4. Give examples to show that objectivity is almost impossible in writing of history.
5. How far do you agree about principles framed by E.P.Cheyney.

Chapter 2: Importance of history and its objectives

History as a teaching subject in schools was introduced long before. It was introduced in the European schools in the sixteenth century. It remained an optional subject for a long time. Students continued its study at will or discontinued it. It was made so much interesting that the burden of other subjects was reduced by its study. In the middle of eighteenth century when history was made compulsory in some schools and memorization of lessons was emphasized interest in it reduced. The element of interest was induced in all school subjects under the influence of Rousseau. Earlier play was a part of history. Now play became a part of of all school subjects thereby reducing the individuality of history.

In the middle of the nineteenth century Karl August Mueller emphasized that history should be a scientific and serious study not merely interesting. He viewed every social activity in historical perspective and showed that the true meaning of all those activities could be understood through a study of history. So, in history narrating merely tales, stories, incidents and events does not serve the purpose of history, but all those things should be narrated as part of process of evolution. If history is taught in this manner students would be able to understand life, society, and good humans in a better way. Mueller had also prepared a complete program of teaching of history.

Prior to him history teaching was done from the point of view of interest. Objectives were set by philosophers and psychologists and to achieve those objectives topics were even modified. A changed version of historical facts was presented and sometimes facts were altogether changed. Mueller was against this approach.

Objectives of history cannot be set by philosophers and psychologists. History has objectives of its own. There is no need to modify or change the facts to achieve those objectives. History will be more interesting and useful if it is objective and nearer truth.

Following is a list of some objectives of history:
- Training of memory, thinking, and power of decision making of students.
- Development of patriotism, good behaviour, and spirit of social behaviour.
- Development of understanding geography and literature with the help of history.
- Development of understanding current events with the help of history.

Above mentioned objectives are of basic importance. There are some objectives of secondary importance. For example:
- Students should get training of searching historical evidence and testimony.
- Students should develop the habit of understanding the true facts.
- They should learn to draw conclusions with the help of facts.
- They should learn to understand the cause and effect of events.
- They should learn to read books in a purposeful manner.
- Their vocabulary should increase.
- They should be helpful in the development of humanism.
- Development of sympathy for neighbouring countries.
- They should learn truthfulness.

There is no doubt that some or even all the above mentioned, objectives can be achieved through other subjects. Some people holding extreme views may even say that teaching of history does not bring any significant change in the education or behaviour of students. But in the absence of research support it would be difficult to say how much other subjects could achieve these objectives. An exact judgement cannot be passed in this regard. It may probably be said that the need of teaching in schools is rather exaggerated, but to say that history should not be taught at all in schools is wrong.

Those who think that history is an extra subject in school curriculum seem to support the ideas of Nietzsche, who says "history has nothing to do in the life of animals. They are not aware of today or tomorrow. Past events do not obstruct their freedom and happiness............human life is obstructed by the increasing burden of the past. It bends, breaks, and diverts it. Children remain happy like animals so long as they do not understand that such and such thing happened in the past. It is in their interest to forget the past happenings. He who cannot forget past cannot be happy, and much worse that he cannot do an activity that makes others happy."

Above mentioned quotation from NIetzsche is true to some extent, and those who want only to look forward and do not want to have a glance backward would appreciate the quotation very much. But it does not happen in practical life. We have to stop and look back the past events and their consequences. It would be bad if somebody starts living in past after reading history, but expert educationalists who want to make history a part of school curriculum do not consider that learning of history would make students lovers of past. New generations after learning history gain some confidence at achieving new things compared to previous generations.

Topics for research are provided to science, social sciences, and literature from their past also. Every subject of study has a history of its own and saying history is a mother of all subjects would not be an exaggeration. We should keep in mind that knowledge of history is essential if we want to understand the present institutions of society, rites and rituals, and cultural diversities of the nation. So, we should make a sincere effort to achieve the objectives of history. Following are objectives of history classified as knowledge, critical thinking, skills, interests, and attitudes:

Objectives of knowledge:
1. Students remember and understand facts, terms, concepts, and events.
2. Students show informative things on maps and charts.
3. Students read and understand information in words, figures, or in any other form.

Objectives of understanding:
1. Students distinguish between facts, events, terms, and concepts.
2. Students distinguish between and compare events, trends, and concepts from one another.
3. Students give examples when explaining events and trends.
4. Students distinguish between important and unimportant events and their cause and effect.
5. Students distinguish between cause and effect, historical directions and destinations.
6. Students arrange events and trends according to their dates.
7. Students point out and correct mistakes in narrations.
8. Students summarize long narrations.
9. Students explain maps, charts, and sources of history.

Objectives of critical thinking:
1. Students identify a problem.
2. Students analyze a problem.
3. Students explain a problem and its possible effects.
4. Students prepare a plan for the solution of a problem.

5. Students search the facts and principles related to the problem.
6. Students establish relationship between facts.
7. Students provide arguments in connection with the facts.
8. Students derive conclusions and generalizations on the basis of facts.
9. Students predict on the basis of conclusions.
10. Students do objective assessment of solution of the problem.

Objectives of skills:
1. Students make historical maps and charts.
2. Students make models.

Objectives of interests:
1. Students collect coins, stones, old scripts etc.
2. Students collect illustrations useful in explaining topics.
3. Students participate in historical drama.
4. Students visit monuments and museums.
5. Students read historical documents, charts, maps.
6. Students write essays on topics of history.

Objectives of attitudes:
1. Students develop sentiments of patriotism.
2. Students develop respect for beliefs, ideas, and styles of living of other people.
3. Students read religions and sects of other people.
4. Students develop friendship with people of other religions and sects.
5. Students follow high ideals.
6. Students respect other cultures.
7. Student accept that every country has contributed in world

civilization.
8. Students help others in civic and social activities.
9. Students accept that nations and countries need help of each other.
10. Students accept that United Nations can help resolve disputes between countries.
11. Students accept that all humans are equal irrespective of religion, sect, race, and colour.

The above mentioned, list of objectives is very long. It has been prepared by the Department of Curriculum and Evaluation of National Council of Educational Research and Training. History teachers can get help and guidance from it and can improve their method of teaching. But it is possible only when they make a conscious effort to achieve these objectives.

Sense of time:

The watches have become so common these days that to talk about sense of time seems to be a little strange. When boys ask someone about time they presuppose that each one has a wrist watch. It also indicates that in our fast moving, life even young boys have a sense of time and responsibility. Children consult time to reach school in time. They keep account of minutes, hours, days, weeks, months. But comprehending account of years and centuries is difficult for them.

History tells us about the rise and fall of dynasties, beginning and end of movements, and contribution of distinguished persons in the evolution of humanity. A simple measure of all these happenings is time. The duration of all these things is measured on the scale of time. So, an important objective of teaching of history is the development of sense of time. Sometimes students cannot appreciate the intensity of a movement due to lack of this sense. They cannot understand that the success of an individual is not due to his efforts alone, but due to past reasons. Those scattered reasons are given a definite shape by a person, thus starting a movement. The knowledge of students about that movement will remain incomplete if they learn the activities of an individual and not the role of other things in building up that movement. Sense of time plays an important role in understanding extended processes of history.

There are two basic elements of sense of time, duration and distance. Duration means the time between the beginning and end of a movement, a dynasty, or a period. Distance means time between present and occurrence of an event in the past, or time between the occurrence of two events in the past. Perhaps we keep in mind "distance and duration" while teaching history, but no conscious effort is made to establish a relationship between "present and past" nor the "occurrence of two events in the past" which may help students to remember the dates of that event. Consequently, students try to keep in mind facts through rote memory and more often forget them soon.

We ourselves can recall that we remember those events and dates which are somehow related to present times, or to the date of an event which we remember due to it being interesting. It is, therefore, necessary that we tell students how much time has passed since the occurrence of an event, or how distant is this event with an interesting event of the past. Such conscious efforts are likely to develop sense of time among students. There may be another exercise for developing sense of time. We may tell the dates of more than one important event and ask students to discuss them changing focus from one to other. This activity may also develop sense of time among students.

Besides, there are some practical exercises which may prove helpful in developing sense of time. One of the exercises is making a timeline. Students may be asked to draw five inches long line and assume one inch equal to fifty years of, say, Mughal rule. The students will show the duration of Mughal king's rule with important events of their times on the timeline. Same exercise can be done with other periods of India and Europe. Two things have to be kept in mind about this exercise. One, the timeline should not be too small. Two, too many events should not be shown on it.

One more type of exercise can be done with timelines. Draw two lines of equal size. One representing a period of Indian history and other a period of European history. Both having almost same beginning and end. Events and their dates can be shown on both lines. This sort of comparing two histories is interesting and informative. Many differences and similarities can be seen and remembered.

Making genealogical charts can also be used as an exercise. Genealogical charts of Kings are easily available in books. Comparison of their birth and death, time of their reign and activities can be done. Genealogical charts of sufis, bhagats, reformers, and other notable persons can be used for this exercise. Genealogical charts prepared by you should not be long.

Dates and events are kept in memory if they are told in association with some interesting event or date. So, student teacher should emphasize historical process instead of telling dates and events in isolation.

Questions:
1. Can history remain a part of school curriculum? Discuss with reference to objectives of history.
2. Discuss the objectives of history for development of skills.
3. Select two topics from class ninth and discuss objectives for the development of attitudes with reference to them.
4. Discuss activities for development of sense of time.

Chapter 3: Method of teaching: Lecture method

Lecture or narration method is generally used for teaching of history in Indian schools. The teacher narrates historical events normally without the help of maps, charts, and pictures. Map is used if easily available and blackboard is used if needed. This method is generally used for transmitting content of history through word of mouth so that students listen more subject matter in less time. It is less expensive and more beneficial. It helps teachers to finish syllabus within academic session. This is the reason why teachers have been using it for so long a time.

A major defect of this method is in putting almost entire burden on teacher in teaching-learning process and neglecting student participation in it. Instead of developing creative abilities of students rote learning is encouraged to pass examinations. Learning process becomes less effective because students are not provided opportunities of thinking, understanding, and discussions. Further, the teacher cannot be sure whether students are really attentive and understanding his lecture or narration. Narrations can be effective if these defects are removed. Some devices are used to make narrations effective. These devices supportive of narration are blackboard, maps, charts, pictures, slides, filmstrips, questions, textbooks, supplementary books, and essays written by students. Let us see how can we make use of these devices in order to make narration method more effective and useful for teaching of history in secondary schools.

We should first be aware with the use of narration since it holds the central position in the method that goes with its name. The first thing is when and why it should be used. It should be used at three times. First, to initiate interest in a topic. It can be very helpful in initiating interest in a lesson at its beginning. Suppose we have to teach the revolt of 1857 we can narrate an interesting event in the beginning of the lesson about Bahadur Shah Zafar, Maharani Laxmi Bai or some other hero of 1857, and then continuing the strategy of developing interest in the lesson narration can be used during the lesson also. Second, narration can be used to explain various reasons for the occurrence of an event. For example, to explain the reason why Napoleon attacked Moscow, because of his ambition, because he wanted to extend the territories of his empire, to crush the ego of Czar of Russia, or to satisfy the thirst of his army for winning victories. These reasons can be explained through narrations. Third, for giving details of events which can hardly be provided by textbooks.

Simplicity and fluency are two specific merits of narration. Teachers who use common words and phrases in narrations are listened with attention. They speak fluently also. But fluency does not depend on simple words alone, command on subject matter is also necessary. Students understand and appreciate a fluent teacher. Teachers who use difficult words fail to transmit subject matter to students.

Questions:

Questions should be asked during, before or after a narration. Questions support narrations. So, we should know the nature of questions to be used at the presentation stage of a lesson. The language of questions should be simple and precise so that listener should have no difficulty to understand them.

Two types of questions are generally asked in history. One, which are asked to test the knowledge of historical facts. For example, what was the relation between Chandragupta Maurya and Ashoka? or which places were conquered by Akbar? Such questions can be found in all textbooks. We test the memory of students with the help of such questions. Two, which help in testing opinions drawn on the basis of facts. Such questions are called "thought provoking questions." These questions spur thoughtfulness and creative power of students. Following is a question of this type: "His end was a piece with his character. If there was a possibility of falling Humayun was not a man to miss it. He tumbled through life and he tumbled out of it." How far do you agree with this statement of a historian? Students may or may not agree with this statement but in both the cases they have to choose the facts, compare them if necessary, and then draw conclusion.

There may be several sub-types of both type of questions. In both types questions of positive or negative response can be asked. Latter type of questions will definitely require thoughtful answers, but in former type questions with positive or negative response are not infrequent. Questions which can be responded by a simple "yes" or "no" are generally not encouraged, but in certain cases no other alternative is possible. Sometimes simple "yes" "no" answers may prove a prelude to thinking. For example, the question- did Akbar really respect Bairam Khan? would possibly be answered by "Yes", but soon after the student will bring to his mind the reasons to justify this answer.

Some questions are asked for the development of lesson. For example, what were the reasons for the French revolution? why did people demand Bahadur Shah Zafar to lead the revolt of 1857? The importance of such questions is that answers of students help the teacher to proceed with the development of lesson.

Use of blackboard

Blackboard beside using for focusing attention of students on important points of lesson is also used to write the summary of the lesson. It is a device that holds its position of importance despite the introduction of new scientific illustrations. So, blackboard should be used as frequently as in the past. Generally, blackboard is used for two purposes. First, to focus attention on a person, place or event. For example, Plassey 1775-should be written on the blackboard when teaching the battle of Plassey, or Reign of Akbar 1556-1605-when teaching Akbar, or the following simple diagram should be drawn on the blackboard when teaching the officers of central government of the Delhi Sultanate:

Offices and Officers of Central Government of Delhi Sultanate
    1. Sadr Us Sudur
    2. Diwane Wizarat
    3. Qaziul Quzzat
    4. Diwane Insha
    5. Arize Mumalik
    6. Diwane Burid

Similarly, to teach why Allauddin Khilji controlled the market the following statement can be given, and following brief can be written on the blackboard: "To keep a large army for stopping the Mongol invasions Allauddin thought to reduce the salaries of soldiers and reduce the prices of commodities, so that commodities could be purchased in lesser salaries"
Problems:
Bigger army
Lesser salaries
Market control
Reduced prices
Such briefs can show the problem and its solution and are easy to remember.

The teacher of history should do practice to draw map of India freehand. This skill will help him show territories of kingdoms, routes of invasions, capitals of provinces etc.

Second, summary of the lesson taught is written on blackboard so that students may note the main points of the lesson. There is a difference of opinion whether summary should be given during the lesson or at the end of it. It is better if the teacher himself decides the time of writing the summary on the board. He can develop the summary with the development of lesson or at the end of it. But in any case, summary should be written in complete sentences.

Textbooks and supplementary books:

Textbooks are used in all methods of teaching history. Lecture or narration are also helped by textbooks. Lessons prepared in Herbartian steps also require help of textbooks. Textbooks are very helpful in project method, Dalton plan, problem solving, and collective recitation. In lecture method textbooks and supplementary books can be read in the classroom, but teachers cannot wholly depend on book readings in the classroom. Readings should be supported by other devices. For example, a teacher may ask a student to read aloud the inscription on the iron pillar at Qutub complex given in the book, but reading will be supported by a short narration to explain the inscription. Textbooks can also be used for showing maps, charts and pictures. Epics like Ramayana, Mahabharata, Iliad, Odyssey can be introduced by reading aloud a stanza from them.

The role of textbook is all the more important outside the classroom. Students write assignments at home and revise lessons taught in the class with its help. Next in importance are supplementary books which can be divided into two categories. Books like: 1) A Short History of Indian People from Earliest Times to the Present Day by Dr. Tarachand, 2) A New History of India by Ishwari Prashad can be placed in the first category, and also books published by N.C.E.R.T. because these are history books as such. The second category of supplementary books contain light historical literature including drama, novel, short stories, and poems. Sir Walter Scott, Charles Dickens, Dennis Wheatley in English, Alexander Duma in French, Abdul Halim Sharar, Nasim Hijazi, Imtiaz ali Taj in Urdu, Kalidas in Hindi are writers of this category. But novel reading should not be encouraged too much.

Slides and Filmstrips

Some topics cannot be taught in history without the help of pictures like buildings, paintings etc. Projectors can be used to show pictures of film strips and slides. Projected pictures may be enlarged to a convenient size and shown from all sides. It is easy to describe them for all pictures need be described.

Questions:
1. How have you read history in school? Write a critical note on it.
2. Give examples to show that questions make narration interesting.
3. What would be the blackboard summary when teaching conquests of Babur?
4. How far do you agree with the use of textbook in teaching history? Which slides would you require while teaching Mughal tombs?

Chapter 4: Method of Teaching: Source Method

Nobody can deny that learning through experience is better in most cases than listening a lecture. We can form an accurate opinion about utensils, ornaments, and other things by seeing them than by simply listening about them. Various architectural features of forts, tombs and other buildings can be appreciated by seeing them compared to listening about them.

Opportunities to learn through direct experience are not many in history, because most material is hidden in the past. Mode of experience is much better but it cannot be used in most cases of historical studies. Its use is possible only in case of visual things. An alternative, though not so exact as in case of buildings etc., can be found in other sources of history. Source method is one such alternative. Can there be a much better means to know the past as provided by letters, edicts, treaties, laws, principles and rules, reports, and books. Let us note here that source method is a method of teaching based on use of sources.

Source method was started in American schools in 1885. Students collected material about events and opinions about them, sifted the reasons for opinions, and then rejecting or accepting opinions. This was the work of higher order, the craft of a full-fledged historian, beyond the ability of a high school student. So, by 1900 this exercise was gradually replaced by source method. Sources are used inside or outside the class for developing interest in history and for developing critical thinking. For developing interest in the subject teacher can read quotations from sources in the beginning and during the lesson. Students get interested after listening that the quotation is from the book written by a person who lived during those times. Take for example the following quotation from Humayun Nama written by Gulbadan Bano (daughter of Babur, sister of Humayun and aunt of Akbar) about the birth of Akbar: "He left his family and other relatives in Amarkot, and made Khawaja Muazzam Nigran (superintendent) of the Haram (royal household). Hamida Banu Begum was pregnant those days. Three days had passed since the departure of the Emperor, on fourth of Rajab Ul Murajjab (seventh month of lunar calendar) on shamba (Friday) at dawn Jahan Panah, Fateh Alam, Jalaluddin Mohammad Badshah e Ghazi was born."

Following quotation from the same source is about the death of Babur: "Next day he (Babur) called all amirs and said: I had entertained for years the desire to handover the throne to Humayun Mirza and start living in a beautiful garden. With the blessing of Allah, I got everything but could not fulfill this desire during my health. Now when disease has made me feeble I want all of you to consider him in my place, be loyal to him, support him with heart and head. I hope Allah Humayun will do good behaviour with you."

When told that these quotations have been taken from the book of Babur's daughter and Humayun's sister students will listen with interest, and also those things told after it. Another way of generating interest in the subject is to find a quotation relevant to an event. The teacher may tell the students that Sher Shah Suri was clear in his mind that a king is the custodian of a country which cannot be partitioned among his relatives like a personal property. He will then ask students to search a quotation from Tarikh e Sher Shahi by Abbas Sherwani which may correspond to Sher Shah's idea of kingship. The Teacher will then project page 38 of the above-mentioned book with the help of overhead projector which contains the following quotation somewhere on this page. "Sher Shah replied that you may tell the khan from me that it is not the country of Roh which could be divided among brothers. The country of Hindustan is ruled by one king---------"

Since the purpose of this exercise is to develop interest in the subject, the teacher himself has to search the source and the relevant quotation, and to arrange an overhead projector to project the quotation.

Two, sources can be used to develop critical thinking. There is much scope in history to alter facts or to give different interpretation to them. Books are available in which facts are very much changed or are interpreted with changed view. Such books create wrong impression on the minds of readers. Since young minds get influenced easily they should be given exercises to judge history with a critical eye. Sources can be of great help in this work. Three exercises are suggested to read books of history or documents with a critical eye. The first exercise is to extract following information about the book or the document:

1. Name of the book and the author.
2. Notable family affairs of the author.
3. Times of his life.
4. Nature of his relations with the raja or the king.
5. Opinions of present day historians about him.
6. His opinion about writing of history.

Above list for collecting information about the author or the book is not complete. Other sundry points may crop up during investigation which may provide important sideline information in this connection. This exercise will help the students to understand that books or documents are written by authors who look at events within their own framework of ideas. So, every event recorded by the author may not be as true or as exact as it appeared to the author and should not be believed blindfoldedly.

The other exercise is for differentiating "facts" and "opinions" in historical writings. The example of fact is: Aurangzeb came to throne in 1658, and the example of opinion is: Jahangir was a justice loving king. For further understanding the difference the following quotation is given again from Humayun Nama of Gulbadan Bano: "From Shahenshah Timur sahib qiran Azam to my Shah Abba (Babur) no prince had ever exerted so much as he. He became king at the age of twelve. On June 10, 1494, and Khutba (sermon) was read in his name in

Andijan, capital of Farghana."

This quotation has two sentences. Gulbadan Bano has given her opinion in the first sentence, and in the other she has given facts. The opinion is true or wrong we know not. Students will identify sentences of fact and opinion by discussing among themselves. Sentences which contain fact and opinion both should not be given to students for exercise. Students are expected to assess with the help of these exercises whether facts are true, partly true or false, and judge opinions critically.

Third exercise is done to compare two books or documents about an event, a building, or a person. Students select similar and dissimilar things in the two books or documents. Following are two quotations about Ibadat Khana located in Fatehpur Sikri. Students will be asked to find common and different facts in the two quotations: "The emperor (Akbar) felt happy since early life in the company of learned and able people. The emperor listened with great interest their discussions on science, religions, sects, ancient and modern history of people, and other things of the world. In the twelfth year of his accession in ziquada (eleventh month of lunar calendar) 982 A.H. (1574) when he came back from Ajmer he gave orders to expert architects and able masons to build in the king's garden a refuge for sufis, and pious men a house in which nobody except high class syed's able ulemas and shaikhs could go --------. It was decided that syeds should sit in the western side, Intellectuals in the southern side, shaikhs and administrators in the northern side officers and courtier in the eastern side."

Tabaqat E Akbari by Nizamuddin Ahmad

"The buildings of Ibadat Khana were complete in 983 A.H. The reason for its construction was that the emperor had won great victories during the last few years--------He had started liking the company of sufis and descendents of Chishtia order, and was involved in conversations regarding Quran and Hadith, and much of his attention was devoted to sufism, science, philosophy, law, and other problems.

After completion of building in which a hall was to be built in all the four sides of it-----------He used to invite every evening of Friday Syeds, shaikhs, officers, and ulemas. But when differences cropped up about seating arrangement Jahanpanah gave orders that officers sit in eastern side, Syeds in the western side, Ulemas in the southern side, and Sheikhs in the northern side."

Muntakhab Ut Tawarikh by Abdul Qadir Badauni.

There are several things common in the quotations:
A. The building of Ibadat Khana started in 982 A.H. and completed in 983 A.H.
B. Its motivation was provided by the company of sufis and pious men.
C. Officers sat in the eastern side, Syeds in the western side, shaikhs in the northern side, and ulemas in the southern side.

Some things are different in the quotations:
A. Akbar's victories were also part of motivations.
B. Separate seating arrangement was due to differences in who should sit where.

Point A in common things has been deduced from both the quotations. Nizamuddin writes that Ibadat Khana building was started in 982 Hijri and Badayuni writes that Ibadat Khana was completed in 983 hijri. So, it is justified to deduce that it started in 982 and completed in 983. These exercises could be done through any books of history, but sources were selected for two reasons. One, to introduce students to sources. Two, even sources have to be viewed with a critical eye what to say about present day books of history.

Question:
1- Which are two objectives for the use of sources of history? Do you agree that critical thinking can develop among students with the help of sources?
2- Explain the method that may develop interest in a lesson and in the subject of history with the help of sources. Write if you can make changes or additions in this method.
3- Select common and different sentences from passages of any two books of history.

Chapter 5: Dalton Plan and Project Method

Dalton Plan

Dalton plan was devised by Helen Parkhurst in Dalton city of American state Massachusetts, hence its name Dalton plan. It became popular in America and England. It is defined as "a system to encourage pupils to learn and develop at their own speed using libraries and other sources to complete long assignments." The school becomes a social center in an easy and effective manner. Its distinct merit is freedom. Student is given freedom to study according to his interest and liking. Its another merit is the cooperation between students in completing assignments. Success of this method depends on keeping continuity in completing assignments. Freedom in respect of speed of each student is emphasized in Dalton plan. But effort is done to maintain individual development along with the development of social consciousness. Its outlines are framed on the basis of the interest of students. Importance is given to student rather than teacher.

Rooms of the school are equipped as laboratories. Books and other material related to one subject are placed in the room. Hence school is reorganized as subject laboratories under Dalton plan. Each laboratory contains books and other material for students of eight to eighteen years of age. The work is assigned to students in the form of an agreement. The agreement contains: name of the work, problems to face, books and quotations to read, practical work to do, duration to finish the work. Students are free to use any laboratory. They may confer with other students. The work done by each student is recorded in graph cards. Some students accumulate their work for the last days of agreed time. The assigned work may or may not be of a specific subject. However, it can be used for history as such, though a class syllabus can hardly be covered by Dalton plan in an academic session.

Following is a specimen of Dalton plan assignment:

Class X

Time 15 days

In the opinion of historian Stanley Lane Poole: "Babur is a link between central Asia and India, between predatory hordes and imperial government, between Timur and Akbar."

Write an essay in the light of the above quotation which may provide answers of the following questions:

1. Do you think that Babur was a man of opposites?
2. How much do you know about the early life of Babur?
3. How will you say that Babur had barbarism of Timur and breadth of ideas of Akbar?
4. Write the conquests of India by Babur.

Following books can be read:

1. Dr.Tara Chand: A Short History of Indian People: From Earliest Times to Present Day.
2. Dr. Ishwari Prashad: A New History of India.
3. Stanley Lane Poole: Medieval India from the Mohammedan Conquest to the Reign of Akbar the Great (History of India No.3)

The above mentioned three books are very old publications and can be doubtfully available in the school library. The quotation about Babur has been taken from the book of stanley Lane Poole. Similarly, original sources are not easily available in schools. So,for this assignment information about Babur can be taken from the medieval period of any book of Indian history..

Following books may also be consulted if available:

1. Tuzke Baburi.
2. Humayun Nama by Gulbadan Bano.

Check your essay if the questions mentioned in the assignment have been answered.

Fifteen days have been allotted to complete this assignment. Students will read books, take notes, and write essay. Evidently, their interest in book reading will increase, will have practice of writing essays. But in the present system of schools it is difficult to adopt this method in the time schedule of schools, and due to urgency to finish syllabus in time, due to paucity of funds, and due to changing behaviour pattern of students. So, complete adoption of Dalton plan is impossible. Only assignments can be given in place of total adoption of Dalton plan in present system of schools. Assignment too, can be occasionally given on topics books on which are available in sufficient number.

Project Method:

Professor W.H.Kilpatrick of Columbia University devised Project method during the time when Dalton plan was devised. The principle behind this method was that children learn by actually solving problems. Kilpatrick was of opinion that we learn only those things which are in use in life. It was not a new idea. Rousseau has written in Emile about the educational importance of practical activities. Froebel has also emphasised planning in connection with education. Few other educationists have also mentioned some activities which are somewhat similar to those of project. Kilpatrick has taught according to project method in an experimental school, and has written much with reference to his experiments.

Kilpatrick has written about two major categories of projects, individual and group projects. All projects are divided into four types: 1) play, 2) story, 3) excursion, 4) handicraft. Projects are purposeful activities. Their purpose becomes clear with the progress of activities. They can be completed in four stages: a) purpose, b) plan c) execution, d) evaluation. They cut subject boundaries. So, technically it is wrong to say that a project is of mathematics or language. But we can give a subject name to a project if more work is done for that subject in that project. More attention is given to that subject in a subject oriented project though it is against the spirit of project method.

Some projects can be used for the subject of history. Following is one such project: It is an excursion type project and its name is "Historical Delhi" Its outlines are given hereunder:

Historical Delhi

Initial statement:

"Delhi is an old historical city. It remained capital of India from ancient to modern times. Places were made capital of north India other than Delhi only a few times.

Delhi has seen rise and fall of several dynasties. Invaders destroyed it and kings founded new cities near its old location. There are not many cities in the world of such historical importance. God knows how many stories are hidden behind its tombs, buildings, and places of worship. People living in Delhi have a good opportunity to visit these buildings and to know about them. Students will gain knowledge and develop abilities after visiting the following places:"

1. Durations of rule of Rajputs, Slave Dynasty, Khilji Dynasty, Tughlaq Dynasty, Syed Dynasty, Lodhi Dynasty, Mughal Dynasty, Prominent kings and their selective achievements of those dynasties.
2. Will draw maps and charts.
3. Will appreciate the architectural characteristics of each period and prepare pamphlets on them.
4. Form a tentative opinion about economic and social conditions of those times.
5. Plan administrative affairs and face related problems.

6. Write essays.

The project can be introduced in different manners, A better way is to introduce it at a suitable opportunity, otherwise pictures of Suraj Kund, Moti Masjid, Shamsi Talab, Qutub minar may be pasted on a flannel board and placed in a corridor where it could be seen by students when coming or going to classes. They would naturally be curious to know about them. Taking advantage of their curiosity following questions will be asked:

1. Which historical places of Delhi have you seen?
2. Where is Suraj Kund?
3. Which buildings are there in Qutub complex?
4. Who has seen Masjid Begumpur?

The purpose of asking these questions is to motivate students to express their willingness and interest to work on this project, and to tell the activities that can be done for this excursion. Following is a list of such activities:

1. Visiting historical places and and observing the features of buildings.
2. Drawing charts, maps, and pictures.
3. Writing essays on the period of buildings.
4. Making models of buildings and collecting their pictures and taking their photos.
5. Making arrangement for vehicles to reach the buildings.
6. Making arrangement for lunch of the group.

After deciding the activities of the project their details will be worked out. Committees will be formed to work out the details and making arrangements. Perhaps a committee will decide the places to visit. Following is a list of places, their location, and dates of their construction. Students can make alteration in this list according to their choices:

Teaching of History in Schools

Number	Monument	Location	Date
1	Suraj Kund	Tughlaqabad	686
2	Iron Pillar	Mehrauli	9 B.C
3	Quwwat Ul Islam Masjid	Mehrauli	1197
4	Qutub Minar	Mehrauli	1206
5	Tomb of Iltutmish	Mehrauli	1235
6	Shamsi Talab	Mehrauli	1229
7	Tomb of Balban	Mehrauli	1286
8	Alai Darwaza	Mehrauli	1310
9	Incomplete Alai Minar	Mehrauli	1311
10	Tomb of Alauddin Khilji	Mehrauli	1317
11	Hauz Khas	Hauz Khas	1295
12	Tomb of Firoz Shah Tughlaq	Hauz Khas	1388
13	Madarsa Firoz Shah Tughlaq	Hauz Khas	1388
14	Ruins of Tughlaqabad	Tughlaqabad	1327
15	Tomb of Ghiyasuddin Tughlaq	Tughlaqabad	1327
16	Firoz Shah Kotla	Delhi Darwaza	1354
17	Ashok ki Laat	Firoz Shah Kotla	265 B.C.

18	Masjid Begumpur	Begumpur	1387
19	Masjid Kalu Sarai	Kalu Sarai	1387
20	Masjid Khirhki	Khirhki	1387
21	Kalan Masjid	Purani Dilli	1387
22	Tomb of Bahlol Lodhi	Chiragh Dilli	1488
23	Masjid Moth	Kotla Mubarakpur	1488
24	Purana Qila	Near Zoo	1541
25	Humayun Tomb	Nizamuddin	1556
26	Jama Masjid	Jama Masjid area	1638
27	Lal Qila	Chandni Chowk	1648
28	Tomb of Safdarjung	Old Airport	1753

Essays can be written on the following topics after visiting these places:
1. Qutub Minar and Masjid Quwwat Ul Islam.
2. Tombs of Mehrauli.
3. Phoolwalon ki Sair.
4. Ruins of Tughlaqabad.
5. Firoz Shah Tughlaq.
6. Masjids built by Khanjahan Firozshahi.
7. Lodhi Sultans.
8. Purana Qila.
9. Humayun Tomb.

10. Shahjahan.

Following maps can be made and photos taken, or pictures collected:
1. Map of Delhi showing places of monuments.
2. Photos of monuments.
3. Masjid Quwwat Ul Islam was expanded several times. A drawing showing Masjid's expansion.
4. A timeline showing reigns of Rajas and Kings with their distinct activities.
5. A model of at least one monument. (Model of Qutub Minar can be made in parts which were contributed by kings).

Following books may help students to read and write about monuments:
1. Asar Us Sanadid by Sir Syed Ahmad Khan.
2. Indian Architecture by Percy Brown.

Arrangement of vehicles to reach the monuments will have to be made. Lunch will also be arranged. Those who have cameras will take them to take photographs of buildings. Besides, services of a professional photographer can also be hired for taking photos to highlight the distinct features of buildings. A committee will make all these arrangements, and will collect money to spend on these arrangements.

All students will jointly prepare a report comprising the details of activities and the benefits accrued by them. An exhibition of the things prepared by students will be arranged. Committee reports will be read in a joint session, and evaluation of the entire work will be done so that shortcomings, merits and demerits will be known to every student, and the report will now be considered complete.

Following are some projects which tend to incline towards history: A house of Shahjahani period, Aryan village, dresses of olden times, Wall of China, old sea galley, forts of defense and residence, Pyramids, street scenes of different times, collection of coins, making a museum, drawing maps, making and collecting copies of edicts and letters, timelines with pictures, collecting specimen of paintings, collecting pictures of Indian temples.

It will now be evident that there is much scope of using projects in history. But it has the same shortcoming as in Dalton plan that this method does not follow our school system and can be used only at opportune times.

Questions:
1- Make a Dalton plan outline of an assignment on the battle of Samugarh.
2- Is it possible to finish the syllabus of secondary classes history by using Dalton plan? Give reasons in support of your answer.
3- Which of the four types of projects is most suitable for history?
4- Plan a project of your choice and write its objectives, introduction, activities and evaluation.

Chapter 6: Curriculum

Selection of facts

Curriculum holds an important position in every subject of study. So, several things have to be kept in mind while framing curriculum. Some of them are related to subject matter and some to psychology. Things related to psychology include age of students, their interests, their likings, their inclinations, and ability to understand. Children cannot be taught things which are beyond their comprehension level. So, while framing curriculum we should keep in mind the age and comprehension level of students, and then think as to what should be taught to them. In other words what facts of history are to be taught. Generally, the curriculum framers arbitrarily include interesting and uninteresting, difficult and easy, all sort of topics in the curriculum. There is no doubt that it is difficult to set standards in history on the basis of which topics could be selected, and perhaps this is the reason of being arbitrary at selection of topics. Still, if efforts are done in organizing the curriculum disorganization and arbitrariness in framing curriculum can be avoided.

Culture Epoch theory of Stanley Hall is the first attempt at framing curriculum. Though it is an old theory but it was applied in history at latter times. Applied as early as eighteenth century its real importance was realized through the experiment of Tuiskon Ziller in 1865. In his opinion childhood and adult age correspond to epochs of culture. Childhood corresponds to the ancient epoch when man lived naked, ate forest fruits; middle age corresponds to middle cultural epoch when man learned to live tribal life; last cultural epoch corresponds to modern age when man made conscious efforts to make life beautiful and orderly. Ziller suggested that ancient period of history should be taught to children; medieval period of history should be taught at middle stage of education; modern period of history should be taught at high stage of education. He prepared a curriculum upto eighth class in which other subjects were coordinated with history at the centre of this curriculum. His experiment was applauded, and many curricula were prepared giving central place to other subjects. Though this theory left its initial charm in years to come, but its effect can still be felt in curricula of history even today.

The other theory that left its mark on history curriculum can be termed as Biographical theory. Carlyle said "behind every achievement in this world can be seen a great man ", and so history can be taught through the lives of great men. Proponents of this theory argue that children up to 13 or 14 years of age are not so mature as to understand cause and effect of historical events. They can understand the success or failure of individuals, but cannot appreciate the process of history, nor can they understand the making or unmaking of institutions. They can be interested in events and conditions, but not in principles and generalizations. So, they emphasized that persons of historical importance should be taught to students at least up to first two stages of school. Biographical theory has its own merits and demerits. A legitimate criticism is that a single individual cannot represent his times. Tolstoy has said "great men serve as labels on historical events". The criticism is convincing in the sense that narrating achievements of great men is quite undemocratic, because in doing so the focus shifts from social life of those times to that person.

Despite criticisms Biographical theory is quite popular and benefits are derived from it at every school stage in the teaching of history. At elementary stage Akbar, Rana Pratap, Sir Syed etc. are read and at higher stage Babur, Jahangir etc. are quoted from their books.

Both these theories provide help not only in framing curriculum but also in the teaching of history as well. A good curriculum is one that provide suggestions for teaching of history also. Both these theories seem to serve this dual purpose. However, attention will be given here to framing of curriculum only. Our first concern is selection of facts.

This problem can be solved in two stages. At the first stage principles should be formed to select facts. At the second stage topics should be selected with the help of those principles. As a part of the first principle of first stage we have to remember that Indian history like all other national histories is a part of world history. The other principle is that the periods of history are characterized by a process, a movement, or a trend. For example, sixth century B.C. is a time of religious regeneration. Buddhism in India, Confucianism in China, and Zoroastrianism in Persia were born in sixth century B.C.

Under the topic of religious regeneration in sixth century B.C. we can include in the curriculum the lives and teachings of Mahatma buddha, Confucius, and Zoroaster. For the sake of convenience, we can name these topics as "Central Idea ". Here the Central Idea is "Religious Regeneration in 600 B.C.", and under it the sub-topics to be taught are: Mahatma Buddha, Confucius, and Zoroaster.

At the second stage these principles will be given a practical shape and the following work will be done:
 a) Search of central ideas.
 b) Topics to be taught under central ideas.
 c) Chronological order of central ideas.

After formulating these principles sources will have to be searched which could help in framing the curriculum. Three sources can be helpful in assisting curriculum framers: syllabuses, textbooks, experienced teachers of history.

1) Syllabuses: are a direct source for framing a curriculum of history. They can give central ideas and topics as such. We can have a score of syllabuses at our disposal from as many states and union territories of India. We need not take syllabuses from all the states and union territories. Four to

six syllabuses will give sufficient variety to make selection from their central ideas and topics.

2) Textbooks: are written to cover the topics given in the syllabus and are rich stores of facts of history. Moreover, they also give an idea about the standard to which a topic may be taught to students. This additional information may be written briefly in the curriculum for the guidance of teachers.

3) Teachers: are a good guide to suggest topics to curriculum framers. We should not take suggestions from experienced school teachers only. University teachers can also give suggestions about a school curriculum. Teachers of school or university can give good suggestions regarding curriculum in the light of their teaching experience not only about topics to be included in a curriculum but also how to teach them.

Following is a part of the syllabus for secondary classes of Jamia Millia Islamia which will further clarify the concept of "central idea" and "topics" to be taught under them:

- Effect of geography on history: Invasions on India, development of civilization in plains
- Human life in pre-history period: Stone age, Metal age.
- Ancient civilizations: India, Egypt, China, Babylonia.
- Aryan people: Social life, Mahabharata, Ramayana, Geeta.
- Religious regeneration in sixth century B.C.: Buddhism, Jainism, Fire Worshipping, Confucianism.
- Roman empire: Democracy, Law.

Organization of Facts:

Teaching of history had started in schools in chronological order. Ancient Indian history was taught in primary classes, medieval history in middle classes and modern history in secondary classes. Chronological order means arrangement of events according to dates usually from last to first. Comenius added topics in this arrangement. An event may also be a topic, but it is used here to denote a movement or a change that has affected history such as French revolution, Crusades, Industrial revolution, American war of independence, Conquest of Constantinople in 1452 or Abraham Lincoln, Mahatma Gandhi. All these topics reflect the thinking and activities of people whether the topic is the name of a person or an event. Organization of these topics should be done chronologically.

There is one more form of this arrangement. It was suggested by Christian Weise. He suggested that history should be taught from present to past, because the objective of history is to understand the present. His regressive approach was much appreciated by J.B.Basedow, and C.G.Salzmann started the study of history from present to past. But regressive syllabus of history was never framed.

Another organization of facts was named "Concentric circles ". These circles represent various stages of school education. The innermost circle represents the first area of knowledge and experience of the beginner, the bigger circle around the first shows the extent of knowledge and experience at a higher stage, and the third circle around both circles shows the status of knowledge and experience at a still higher stage. The proponents of concentric circle organization suggested to divide school education in three stages, and the course of history in three parts. Parts of the course should be allotted to parts of the stage. The course taught in part one at stage one should be repeated in brief at stage two along with new topics of part two, and previous topics of part one and two should be repeated in brief at stage three along with new topics of stage three. This way courses of history will be repeated at every new stage along with new topics of that stage.

The idea of concentric circles was the outgrowth of the approach of Pestalozzi and the educational thinking of Rousseau. In 1820 the concentric circles approach became so popular in Europe that history syllabuses were framed on the pattern of concentric circles. French schools adopted it in 1852 and discharged it in 1865. Concentric circle syllabuses became quite popular in American schools also. In the last decade of the nineteenth century American history was taught in eight classes of elementary schools with additional topics in each higher class. But it was a wearisome process. So, after some time American syllabuses were framed afresh.

In Indian schools teaching of history starts at primary stage as a part of social studies. It is taught in the form of stories. At middle stage continuous historical narration is introduced by adding new facts. In secondary classes continuous historical narration is maintained with cause and effect of events thereby making it more meaningful and realistic.

Chronological and concentric circles can be used together in an organization of facts. Syllabus of history can be divided chronologically into primary, middle, and secondary stages. Central ideas and topics assigned to primary stage will be briefly revised at middle stage along with the topics assigned to it, and the topics of the secondary stage and a brief summary of earlier two stages will be assigned to the secondary stage.

Questions:
1- Which theory among the culture epoch and biographical do you like more? Give arguments in favour of your answer.
2- Which of the sources for selection of facts you like more, and why?
3- What do you understand by chronological arrangement.? Frame a part of syllabus for eighth class in chronological order.
4- Discuss concentric circles organization.

Chapter 7: Textbook of History

When a book is considered suitable for a class it is prescribed as a textbook for that class. But the selectors of textbook have always a question mark as to the criteria which could help to assess the suitability for a particular class. This work is generally done with the help of syllabus. Books that come up to the standard of a class are prescribed for that class. But now when the practice of writing books according to the requirements of syllabus have become common among writers of books age and abilities of students are kept in mind. Chapters, exercises, and questions are arranged according to the principles of education and psychology of students thereby making textbook more suitable and useful for them.

History books are no exception to this process and the principles observed in writing books for other subjects are also observed in the case of history books at the time of writing or selecting them as textbooks. The first principle to be observed is of national integration. India is composed of different cultures, sects, languages, and religions. People of different colour and race inhabit here. India has emerged for the first time as a political entity after independence. The concept of Indian nationhood is not so clear as of the European nations. So, it is essential for people of India to maintain the solidarity of their country despite its diversities. The country belongs to its people. People's prosperity is linked to country's prosperity. If people are hardworking and honest the country will definitely develop. So, national development should be given precedence over multifarious diversities of people. This sentiment can develop Indian nationalism, and people may think in terms of nationhood instead of their differences. History can help a lot in the development of this sentiment.

Some people may have the doubt that this principle will affect the objectivity of history. It is not true. Accepting this principle does not mean that facts of history would be presented in a distorted form. Facts cannot be changed but care should be taken not to highlight differences at the time of giving opinion on them. The opinion which the author thinks correct should not be changed for fear of hurting the feelings of a community or else history will be lost to propriety.

Other principle in this connection is that content of history should be in consonance with the current trend in history and should help in the achievement of its present objectives. The histories written so far are mostly political in nature. But in the last few years much has been written on the social, economic, and cultural aspects of history. Writers or scholars of history of textbooks should keep in mind that content should cover all these aspects of history. In doing so all those human activities and achievements will come to light which were left unwritten considering them unimportant, but without them full mental picture of past times cannot be drawn.

Teaching of history is not for students to learn some facts of history, but to think in a specific way; they should reach conclusions with the help of arguments and proofs; they should develop critical thinking; they should adopt values which were cherished in all times; their behaviour should be looked at with approval. All these things are possible when they understand the propensities of history, and succeed in achieving its objectives.

The third principle in this connection is that subject matter is presented by keeping the psychology of students in view. There are some psychological principles governing the learning of new things. Those principles apply on history also. First psychological principle is clarity of objective. If it is clear in the mind of a learner, why he has to learn a new thing he will do maximum effort to learn it; proper motivation increases the desire to know every new thing. Second psychological principle is to relate new things to old things. There are some more principles which writers and selectors of textbooks should keep in mind. They are: from easy to difficult, from real to imaginary, from observation to argumentative.

It should be reiterated here that textbook writers and selectors should keep in mind the age and abilities of their readers, especially in the use of language and presentation. Difficult words and phrases should be avoided as much as possible. Simple and common words and phrases increase the beauty of language and presentation of subject matter, and the reader reads the book with interest. Pictures, charts, and maps should be used wherever necessary. Illustrations not only help in explaining things but increase interest in the book also.

Other principle is that subject matter, exercises, and other things should be so arranged in the textbook as to help the teacher in teaching them. Textbooks are generally written from the point of view of students and there is seldom any guidance for teachers. Teachers do not get suggestions as to what changes can be done in their method of teaching and how to improve it. If there are direct or indirect suggestions for teachers, they can make changes in their method of teaching. For example, what type of assignments they can give, which monuments they can show, and what information they can give about them.

In the last writers and selectors should remember that high priced books are not suitable for our schools and admitting the importance of pictures, charts, maps etc. price of books should be kept within the reach of students.

History Teacher:

History teacher like all other subject teachers should know his subject well. It is possible when he regularly studies it. History is a vast subject full of facts. To expect from an individual that he would remember if not world history at least history of his own country would be a folly. History teacher should realize himself also that he cannot remember the entire history of his country. So, he should focus attention on one period of national history. Naturally he would focus attention on a period of his interest. In depth study of a period will discipline his ideas and he will understand the process of history. He will learn to derive conclusions on the basis of facts. Thus experience gained from the study of one period will be utilized for other periods. His teaching will be benefitted with this experience.

Teachers can take advantage from research in his study of a period. Historical research is a process in which relevant documents, letters, and books are consulted, conclusions are drawn and generalizations made. A researcher knows, of course, with the help of other experts, where can he obtain material relevant to his problem. In short, his indepth study of a period will introduce him to elements of historical research, which will ultimately help him in improving the quality of his teaching, and in developing critical thinking.

A teacher of history should be familiar with world history because of two reasons. One, as told earlier that every national history is part of world history. Two, its study will give breadth to his ideas. He will know that many things were common in early civilizations and Indian civilization was not something very different.

Study of Anthropology will also give answers to some basic questions which will help teacher of history in improving his teaching. For example, the age of first human habitation, number of stages before reaching the stage of civilization, original human races, making of clans and families.

There is much scope of difference of opinion in history, the teacher should hold his opinion in abeyance during such differences. Students should be allowed time to collect material regarding the disputed opinion and then to reach a studied opinion. The teacher then gives his own opinion on the disputed problem. The teacher should maintain the role of a moderator during such discussions.

Many people have not a clear concept of method of teaching. It is not something mysterious. Methods taught in training colleges are neither sacrosanct nor unchangeable. Every method does not match with the personality of every teacher. Every method changes a little when used by a teacher. Most common is lecture method. Each one of us has listened several lectures during college education. Some of them were good and others not so good because they were delivered by different lecturers. If you think that your method needs a change you can change it at points which are making it ineffective.

Questions:
1- Which merits and demerits will you judge in a textbook for class eighth?
2- How will you write in a textbook about a disputed problem of history?
3- Write the qualities of history teacher. Write briefly.
4- Which method of teaching will you use as history teacher so that correct attitudes develop in your students?

Chapter 8: Evaluation in History

Beginning of evaluation started the day when man assessed his deeds. Perhaps it began with the advent of man on the earth. But examination as we understand it today also started long ago. Knowledge of students was tested in a discussion in Nalanda university in seventh century BCE. Discussion was the mode of examination those days. Perhaps same mode of examination was in practice in Taksala and Vikramshila universities also. Testing was done at the time of admission in medieval European universities and the same method was adopted in schools. Examination took different forms in changing times till it took the present form of written examinations.

There are three types of examinations, observational, oral, and written, and three standards to judge the performance of examinees. Following are the three standards against which performance of examinees is judged:
1. Examiner's own mental standard.
2. Group standard.
3. Individual standard.

Performance in essay type examination is generally assessed on the first standard. Examiner makes a mental answer for every question and award marks on its basis. Some examiners use second standard. They pick up the best and the worse answers of a question of the group, and judge answers on their basis. Third standard is used on the performances of an individual, whether he has improved or not on the previous performance. The choice of standard will be determined by the examiner. He can use two instead of one standard in his assessments.

Testing in history could be written, oral, or through observation depending upon the nature of objectives. Objectives related to behaviour can be tested through observation. Objectives related to attitudes given in chapter two can be judged by observing the behaviour of students.

Oral testing is generally considered a part of written testing. Oral testing is suitable at elementary stage. It can be used as a part of written examination at middle and secondary stages. Oral testing should not be conducted without preparation.

Written examinations are used more than any other mode of examination. Questions in essay type examination should be so formed as to assess answers objectively. They should be clearly worded and precise. Questions of objective nature have been introduced for objective assessment on the knowledge of students

Types of objective questions:

A. Alternate choice: A sentence is given in these questions. Students mark it right or wrong as the case may be. Sometimes the answer may be given "yes" or "no".
   Following are examples of alternate choice questions:
   1. Chanakya was the mahamantri of Ashoka_____.
   2. Akbar did not give the proof of his political wisdom by abolishing Jazia_____.
   3. Third battle of Panipat was fought between Marathas and Ahmad Shah Abdali_____.

B. Completion type: Incomplete sentences with an empty space for completion of sentences is left.
   Following are examples:
   1. _____ became nawab of Bengal after the execution of Siraj Ud Daula.
   2. Pitt's India Act was passed in_____.
   3. _____ was the first Viceroy of India.

C. Multiple choice: A statement followed by three or four choices is given. One of the choices is correct.
   Following are the examples:
   1. Duration of Hiuen Tsang's stay in India:
       a. 12 years.
       b. 14 years.
       c. 16 years.
       d. 18 years
   2. Shah Jahan rose in rebellion against Jahangir because:
       a. Jahangir did not like him.
       b. Jahangir wanted to send him to Deccan.
       c. Nurjahan wanted Shaharyar to be next king.
       d. Shah Jahan refused to go on Qandhar campaign.
   3. Akbar's fame is different from other Mughal rulers because:
       a. He was a great conqueror.
       b. Pomp and pageant of his court was more than other rulers.
       c. He found new towns and made grand buildings.
       d. He integrated various sects and creeds to make a stable empire

In multiple choice type besides correct answer the other options are called distractors. Distractors should be as near the correct answer as possible.

D. Matching Type: In these questions two lists are given opposite each other. The lists do not have a specific arrangement. Events, names, achievements are given in the first list which are matched with dates given in the opposite list having numbers. The numbers are then written with matched events on empty lines given in the first list. Following is an example of matching type:

Accession of Iltutmish-------	1-	1221
Death of Sultana Razia------------	2-	1287
Death of ghyasuddin Balban------------	3-	1211
Attack of Changez Khan on India-------	4-	1240
Iltutmish came to throne------	5-	1200

Iltutmish came to throne in 1211, so 3 will be written on the empty space given at that event. Sultana Razia died in 1240, so 4 will be written on the empty space given at that event. Ghyasuddin Balban died in 1287 and Changez Khan attacked India in 1221, so 2 and 1 will be written on the empty spaces of those events.

There is no limit of writing number of things in two lists. But if the lists are too long matching will become difficult. So, ten things in both the lists will be sufficient. One extra number can be given in one list, as given in the above example.

E. Arrangement Type: this type of questions are quite suitable for history. Events or individuals are arranged date-wise in this type of questions.

Following is an example of arrangement type:

Arrange the following persons according to their date of birth. Arrangement should be from old to young:

1. Babur
2. Nadir Shah
3. Shivaji
4. Akbar
5. Jahangir

The arrangement will be: 1, 4, 5, 3, 2. A modification can be done in this type of questions.

For example: main events during the reign of Aurangzeb can be shown on a time line.

The events are: accession of Aurangzeb, death of Shah Jahan, death of Shambhuji, death of Aurangzeb, Shivaji's attack on Surat.

First a scale for timeline will be made i.e.1 inch = 5 years and then date of events will be collected and written on the timeline. Though much time will be spent on this exercise, but it would help students to remember dates.

Item Analysis:

A great advantage of objective type testing is that questions (or items) can be easily analyzed, and it can be found that a question is suitable or not for a particular class. This thing can be technically said that a particular question is sufficiently difficult or not for a class and can discriminate or not between fast and slow students of that class. If a question has both these virtues it is considered suitable for that class. In objective type tests suitability of a question for a class can be determined with the help of item analysis. Item analysis can be understood with the help of the following example:

Suppose there are 28 students in a class. They are given a question paper of 100 marks. There are 100 questions in the paper, so each question is of 1 mark. Correct answers are marked right, and incorrect answers are marked wrong. After awarding marks on all the answer papers they are arranged in the order from highest to lowest total marks. The names of students and marks obtained by them item wise are tabulated in a table as given below:

S.No	Student	Item No.	Item No.	Item No.	Total
1	Mahmood Ali	R	R	R	79

Teaching of History in Schools

| 2 | Masooda Begum | W | W | R | 72 |
| 3 | Usha Kumari | R | W | R | 65 |

Since there are 28 students in the class in the table there will be 28 names and there will be 100 items. Marks will be tabulated in 100 columns and totals will be written in the last column. The first nine will be the fast students and the last nine will be the slow students. In the table below the marks of only fast and slow students have been taken into account:

I.N.	C.A. of F. & S.	Dif. Val (F+S)/ Both Grs. X100	Dis. Val (F-S)/ One Gr. X100	Sel. Or Rej.
1	F = 8 S=4	(8+4)/18 X100 67%	(8-4)/9X100 44%	Selected
2	F=2 S=2	(2+2)/18X 100 22%	(2-2)/9X100 0%	Rejected

Abbreviations in the formula:
I.N.= item number; C.A.=correct answer; F=fast; S=slow; Dif.Val.=Difficulty value; Dis.Val.=Discrimination value; Gr.=group of students.

Selected items are considered suitable for the class. Rejected items are improved and again tested through item analysis. Items between 25% and 75% have sufficient difficulty value, and items more than 20% have good discrimination value.

Questions:
1- What are the standards of examining the essay type answers? Which of them is better?
2- How far do you agree that essay type testing is very necessary for history?
3- How many objective type questions? Which type do you like most?
4- Write briefly item analysis?

Chapter 9: Preparation of Lesson Plan; Some Specimen Lesson Plans

Teachers normally do some mental preparation before going to class. They sometimes write short notes about the lesson. But under training teachers who have no, or very little experience of classroom teaching have to prepare rather detailed lesson plan before going to class. They should enter the class with a clear head to face the class and to communicate with ease and poise.

Student teachers think that a lesson should be taught exactly according to the plan. But it is not true, because a plan may be changed in the classroom due to some unforeseen conditions. A plan should be flexible enough to change during its development due to requirements of students. This change could be done in the arrangement of teaching points or because of some questions of students which may necessitate further explanation of his planned explanations. Some students are more intelligent than the expectations of teachers. Answers to their questions cannot be given within the framework of plan. They are satisfied only with detailed explanations.

Another important thing is that a student teacher should be well prepared with the subject matter. His knowledge of the subject matter should not be limited to textbook alone, but he should have studied books of higher standard or contemporary sources. Besides, he should have updated knowledge of modern teaching methods.

It has been noticed that student teachers who are well versed in subject matter make changes in their teaching method if need be. Teaching method and subject matter are so much near each other that if one is weak the other automatically becomes weak. So, unless command over subject matter is not strong change in teaching method can seldom be affected.

Third thing in this connection is that student teacher beside knowing his students in general should know them individually. The more he is aware of the likings, interests and psychological needs of his students more effective his teaching will be, and he will plan his lessons more on psychological considerations. His plans will include questions, illustrations and activities according to the mental standard of students.

The last thing in this connection is that his plan should have variety of work. The lesson should not be confined to a process of speaking and listening only. Students should do variety of things as listening, questioning, narrating on their own, searching places on the map, and writing notes. If the lesson is composed of various activities the class will not have that boring atmosphere which is witnessed during some history lessons when students are mere listeners and are not actively participating in the development of lesson.

Specific Steps of Lesson Plan:

Most lessons are planned on the formal steps of Herbart. Though formal steps are considered outdated and not coming up to the modern psychological principles of education. But it would be difficult to deny that formal Herbartian steps are considerably realistic and enough flexible, and whenever new planning steps are devised these steps may be partly but assuredly join them. Since we do not want to join a discussion about how old is the philosophy of education of Herbart and how much does it correspond to modern psychological principles we will consider only the steps of plan which are generally approved and are prevalent.

Most important in the lesson plan is objective. The lesson has to be taught for the development of knowledge and understanding or for skills and attitudes. There may be lessons in which communication of knowledge and development of understanding is necessary and in some emphasis is laid on attitudes. There may be some lessons in which knowledge and skills are specific objectives. Variety of lessons have variety of objectives. A long list of objectives is given in chapter two which contains objectives of knowledge, understandings, skills, and attitudes. That list is of general objectives of history. These objectives when used for the achievements and activities of a particular person or for development of particular skill or attitude it is called specific objective. Specific objective is generally of a particular lesson. For example, in that list first general objective is that students should understand and keep in memory facts, terms, concepts, and events. Teaching Akbar's conquests this general objective will be reduced to this specific objective "students should be able to understand and keep in mind the conquests of Akbar and their cause and effect", and the specific objective related to skill will be "students should be able to show on the map of India the places and years of conquests."

After settling the objectives, the work of selection and organization of subject matter starts. In the light of objectives, it is decided which facts are to be taught, how much emphasis has to be given on each of them, and what should be their arrangement. Along with it is also decided how to present an event either through discussion, through narration, through question, or through a practical work. Selection of subject matter and its organization helps in deciding the modes of motivation and illustrations to be used. Coins, tombstone or pillar writings, pictures, charts, models etc. can be used for this work. They not only motivate but clarify concepts also.

The last step in the lesson plan is recapitulation. It is often done through questions. Its purpose is to assess the extent to which students have learned the things taught to them, what conclusions they have drawn; have they understood the importance of problems under study. Since most history lessons are related to imparting knowledge and developing understandings questions are asked to evaluate them.

Regarding skills and attitudes evaluation can be done through observing students in their practical work.

Lastly "homework" should be given for revising the lesson and preparing them for the next lesson. But homework should not be a time-consuming exercise.

Few specimen lesson plans are given in this chapter

Lesson Plan 1

Class: X
Time: 40 minutes

Topic: Background of the First World War.

Specific Objectives:
1. Nationalism is essential to integrate the people of a country. But when this sentiment produces hatred and aggression between countries it becomes dangerous.
2. When science became a toy in the hands of imperialism and nationalism so many people and so much property were destroyed that such a destruction had never taken place.
3. Students should hate war and collision because they destroy the culture and civilization.
4. Students should be able to show on a map of Europe countries that were party to the First World War.

Material Aid: A map of Europe of 1914.

Introduction:
1. Which events occurred between 1962 and 1965?
2. India was at war with which countries on those years?
3. Which countries of the world are arrayed against each other nowadays?
4. Which countries were a party to the First World War?

Statement of Aim: Let us read today about the First World War. Why it was fought, and which countries fought it.

Presentation:
      Germany defeated France in 1871 and annexed Alsace Lorraine,

and forced France to pay as indemnity of war hundred billion dollars. These conditions were very harsh. Germany had the fear of retaliation by France. In order to forestall such eventuality Germany entered into a triple alliance with Austria, Hungary, and Italy. France countered by entering into an alliance with Britain and Russia. Thus, European powers were divided into groups. Tension built up and the atmosphere was ripe to explode into a war.

Questions:
1- Which countries were members of German triple alliance?
2- Who was then the chancellor of Germany?
3- Why were such alliances made?

Since such alliances are based on mutual fear preparations of war accompany them. Recruitment in army starts, arms are manufactured, and entire national energy is spent on meeting the future danger. Minds of people get ready to coming war. All this happened in Europe before 1914. Germany left behind Britain and France in arms race. Its arms were modern and dangerous. Germany increased its naval power also because of its awareness that Britain and France take much advantage of their naval powers.

Question:
1- How is naval power used in war?

Britain and France were imperial powers. Many countries of the world were under their political or economic control. They were either ruling those countries or had made them markets for their products. They were earning much wealth and spending it on their people who lived a life of plenty and comfort. Germany also wanted to become an imperial power and to improve the standard of life of its people. Since many countries were already under the control of Britain and France Germany had to face them in its bid to become an imperial power. Therefore, rivalries between them had been continuing for a long time.

Questions:
1- What do you understand by imperialism?
2- Why Germany wanted to be an imperial power?
3- Show on the map locations of Germany, France, and Britain.

To unite German nation and to generate feelings of superiority in them the rulers of Germany started a propaganda that German nation is better than other nations of Europe. German rulers did this propaganda so well that German people believed it. They became proud of themselves and looked down upon other nations of Europe. Sense of belonging to one's country is a good thing; this is what we call nationalism. But when this sentiment under rate other nations it is not only bad but often very dangerous. The danger of war increased several times more under this propaganda.

Questions:
1- What did German rulers do to unite German people?
2- What type of misguided national sentiments can be dangerous?
3- Show Britain on the map of Europe and state which power can defend it most?

Recapitulation:
1- Name the countries which entered into alliance against Germany?
2- What status Germany wanted to attain against France and Britain?
3- What do you understand by nationalism?
4- Do you think the measures taken by the German people from the point of view of defense were right or wrong?

Homework: Write the names of heads of government of countries which were at war in the First World War.

Lesson Plan 2

Class IX
Time 40 minutes

Topic: Beginning of Freedom Movement in India

Specific objective:
1- Students will be aware of the beginning of freedom movement in India.
2- Students will know that great men developed the sentiments of freedom among the people directly or indirectly during this period.

Material aid:
Pictures of Radhakant Dev, Swami Dayanand, Raja Ram Mohan Roy, Keshav Dev Sen, Ramkrishna Paramhans, Ishwar Chand Vidya Sagar

Introduction:
1- How many years have passed since India got independence?
2- Name some people who helped in getting independence?
3- What do you know about Gandhiji?
4- When did independence movement start?

Statement of Aim: The desire for independence had started long before, earlier than the birth of Gandhiji. We will read today about the people who watered the plant of freedom before the birth of Gandhiji. We will read about the period when the desire of freedom had still not become a movement.

Presentation:

1- The attitude of the English people was ingrained in their superiority. They thought they were superior to Indians culturally and politically.

   Question: Was the British attitude of superiority justified in your opinion?

2- Indian reaction to this attitude was of two types. One, was that Indian culture was better. Radhakant Dev and Swami Dayanand were prominent persons holding this view. Pictures of Radhakant Dev and Swami Dayanand will be shown here. Second type were Raja Ram Mohan Roy and Keshav Dev Sen who favoured English culture. Pictures of Raja Ram Mohan Roy and Keshav Dev Sen will be shown here.
   Question: Whose reaction was right in your opinion?

3- East India Company finished local industries and created a new class of Zamindars who supported the British.
   Question:
   1) What was the attitude of Zamindars?
   2) What, in your opinion, could be the attitude of local industry owners?

4- Liberal ideas were generated by English education and western mode of thought. This liberalism filtered down to common people and they started thinking on these lines.
   Question: What does democracy mean?

5- Raja Ram Mohan Roy represented the liberal people of his times. He emphasized English education, prohibition of Sati, Casteism, and tried to modernize Hinduism. His movement is famous as

Brahmo Samaj. Raja Ram Mohan Roy was in favour of freedom. Question: Do you agree with the views of Raja Ram Mohan Roy regarding English education.

6- Different organizations were also party to generate feelings of nationalism as Theosophical society, Rama Krishna mission, Arya Samaj. Pictures of Ramakrishna Paramahansa and Ishwar Chandra Vidyasagar will be shown.

7- Educated Indians became familiar with new ideas after learning English language.

8- Many researchers of Indian culture unveiled the virtues of Indian culture. Among them are included Bhandarkar, Har Prashad Shastri, Ranade, and Max Mueller.

Recapitulation:
1. Which reason seems to be more important in developing the desire for Freedom?
2. Why Raja Ram Mohan Roy is considered the best representative of his times?
3. Why English language is given so much importance in this connection?

Homework: Collect the pictures of all those persons you have read about and write five lines on each of them.

Lesson Plan 3

Class IX
Time 30 minutes

Topic: Difference between Fact and Opinion

Specific objective: Students will be able to read books of history with a critical eye.

Material Aid: A short passage from the Ain e Akbari of Abul Fazl will be cyclostyled and distributed among students.

First stage: Since it is the first exercise of its nature following questions will be asked to differentiate between Facts and Opinions. In case of no response from the students the teacher will himself tell them difference between sentence of facts and sentences of opinion.

Sentences of Facts:
1- Taj Mahal was built by Shah Jahan.
2- Akbar was born in Amarkot.

Sentences of Opinions:
1- Taj Mahal is the most beautiful building of the world.
2- The reason for the success of Akbar was the wisdom of his court advisers.

Second stage:
When teacher is confident that students have understood the difference between the sentences of facts and opinions the cyclostyled passage of Ain e Akbari will be distributed among them and to test whether they

have understood the passage following questions will be asked:

"I thought in the beginning to narrate the achievements, virtues, and experiences, because of which they reached such a high position. But I do not want only to praise them. It does not behove the adviser of the king to praise others. And my truthfulness also does not allow me to write only the things of praise and to keep silence on disapproved things.

So, I will only write the names and titles of people:
1. Noble of ten thousand mansab: Prince Salim, eldest son of Jahanpanah (refuge of the world) the king.
2. Noble of eight thousand mansab: Prince Sultan Murad, second son of Jahanpanah (refuge of the world) the king.
3. Noble of seven thousand mansab: Prince Sultan Danyal, third son of Jahanpanah (refuge of the world) the king.

Akbar had five sons:
1. Hasan
2. Husain, (twin brothers, 3 Rabi ul awwal 972 Hijri, lived only three months)
3. Sultan Salim (Jahangir)
4. Sultan Murad
5. Sultan Danyal.

I hear names of three daughters:
1. Shahzadi Khanam 977 Hijri, born three months after Sultan Salim
2. Shukrunnisa Begum whose marriage took place in 1001 Hijri with Mirza Shahrukh
3. Aram Banu Begum. Both these daughters were born after the birth of Sultan Danyal." - AineAkbariAbul Fazl

Questions:
1. Who has written this passage?

2. How many sons had Akbar?
3. How many daughters had he?
4. What was the name of his son-in-law?
5. What is the name of the book from which this passage has been taken?
6. Why has Abul Fazl said that he did not want to tell the achievements of prominent people of the court?
7. If you write about the noble people of your times would you say the same thing?

Third stage: Teacher will ask students to underline the sentences of facts. Students will decide after discussion which sentences are really of facts. Similar exercise will be done for sentences of opinion.

Role of Teacher: Teacher will start discussions at this stage. He will keep the discussion at moderate level, and will announce the decision at the end of discussion. Model discussion would be in which teacher takes less part in it, and students themselves reach the decision. Teacher will have to decide himself at which time to join discussion or abstain from it.

Chapter 10: Communalism and Writing of History in Modern India

Books of history have been written in India for a long time. Innumerable books of history have been written during the medieval period which are helpful in drawing real picture of that period. It would not be wrong to say that historians of that period emphasized the deeds of kings, generals, and nobility. Therefore, most histories of that period are political in nature. Still there are some histories which help in knowing the economic, social, and cultural life of that period. Ain e Akbari of Abul Fazl and Muntakhab Ul Lubab of Hashim Khafi Khan can be named in this connection. Social life of pre-medieval period is best known through religious books like Ramayana and Mahabharata.

The art of history writing got a new life after the advent of the British. English people greatly influenced the educated people of India and opened new channels of thought. People started thinking how history should be written. Some people thought that ancient was an exemplary period, so it should be eulogized. Some who were happy with the governance of English people because they had saved them from autocrats considered their period exemplary. Third school of thought was composed of those people who had risen in the wake of freedom movement. They considered the past times better than the present English period. For them medieval and ancient were better periods.

Max Mueller's name can be placed at the top of the list who considered ancient as an exemplary period. His country was Germany. He had deep knowledge of Sanskrit language, and was very much impressed by Vedas. He has translated Rig Veda into English. Getting impressed by the enthusiasm of Max Mueller many historians started thinking on his lines. So, ancient period which was hidden behind the thick curtain of times started coming out. But the wrong happened when extremists thought it a model period and started eulogizing every single point of that period. Impressed by this point of view historians wrote books which were liked by those who did not want to fulfill the demands of changing times.

    The leader of the second school of thought was James Mill. In his book "History of British India" he divided Indian history into Hindu culture, Muslim culture, and English culture. This division of history was so much liked that ancient, medieval, and modern periods became Hindu, Muslim, and British periods. James Mill thought that English period was a period when people were provided maximum facilities, and so it was much better than the earlier two periods when autocrat kings ruled over India.

    These ideas were naturally very much liked by the ruling class of the English people. So, many high officers of the British administration turned into historians. Secretary, Foreign Affairs Sir Henry Meier Elliot selected Persian histories of medieval India, got them translated into English, and published them in 1867. This history covers eight volumes and is titled "History of India as Told by Its Own Historians- Mohammedan Period ". Selected parts in it promote communalism. Some extremist historians having impressed by these histories started seeing history through communal glasses. Since Persian histories were not translated into English on such a large scale these histories remained under study of English knowing historians for a long time, and are consulted even now.

    The origin of freedom movement can be traced back in the last years of the nineteenth century. Such a great public movement had never occurred in the history of India. Children and old men everybody came under its influence. Students of history could not remain unaffected by it. The movement gave birth to historians who believed in the grand traditions of the past. James Mill's division of history was already in public. So, ancient and medieval periods were eulogized as

Hindu and Muslim in order to compensate the deprivations of past. The period of freedom movement was of political activities. People used to become emotionally charged within no time. The period was of extremism, and to continue the movement such extremism was necessary and legitimate. So, the historians of that period are not so objective as they ought to be.

But it would be wrong to understand that every historian and student of modern India was so much affected by any one of the three trends and presented history in an unscientific manner. The art of historian is based on research and investigation. He assesses the proof and analyse the events very critically before arriving at conclusions. This art was fully known to the historians of modern India. So, quite a few historians of this period cannot be called unscientific.

For detailed discussion on this topic see the following book: Romila Thapar: Communalism and Writing of Indian History, Peoples Publishing House, Delhi, 1969.

www.ingramcontent.com/pod-product-compliance
Lightning Source LLC
LaVergne TN
LVHW041635070426
835507LV00008B/647